MAGICIAN'S HAT

OTHER BOOKS BY BILL TREMBLAY

CHAPBOOKS

A Time for Breaking (Yellow Bus Press, 1970)
Stop the Violence (Four Zoas Press, 1978)

POETRY

Crying in the Cheap Seats (University of Massachusetts Press, 1971)
The Anarchist Heart (New Rivers Press, 1977)
Home Front (Lynx House Press, 1978)
Second Sun: New & Selected Poems (L'Epervier Press, 1985)
Duhamel: Ideas of Order in Little Canada (BOA Editions Ltd., 1986)
Rainstorm Over the Alphabet: Poems 1990-2000 (Lynx House Press, 2001)
Shooting Script: Door of Fire (Eastern Washington University Press, 2003)

NOVELS

The June Rise: The Apocryphal Letters of Joseph Antoine Janis
(Utah State University Press, 1994; reissued Fulcrum Publishing, 2001)

MAGICIAN'S HAT

poems by
Bill Tremblay

Lynx House Press
Spokane, Washington

ACKNOWLEDGMENTS

"Panic Breathing" was published in *The Quint* (Canada) Vol. 2, #4.
"A Square in Valencia" was published in *The Planet Formerly Known as Earth* (January, 2011).

Personal thanks to all those who helped during the writing: Phillip Garrison, who started me on the path of this book; Floyce Alexander; Jack Martin; Ted Lardner; Christopher Howell; Frank Fetters; Thom Ward; Michael Robeson; and, of course, always, Cynthia.

Cover Art: *Self-Portrait 1948* by David Alfaro Siqueiros. National Gallery of Art; used by permission.
Author Photo: Cynthia Tremblay
Book & Cover Design: Christine Holbert

FIRST EDITION

LIBRARY OF CONGRESS CATALOGING-IN-PUBLICATION DATA

Tremblay, Bill.
    Magician's hat : poems on the life and death of David Alfaro Siqueiros / by Bill Tremblay.—
First edition.
        pages cm
    ISBN 978-0-89924-129-6 (alk. paper)
1. Siqueiros, David Alfaro. 2. Mural painting and decoration, Mexican. 3. Mural painting and decoration—20th century. 4. Art and revolutions—Mexico. I. Title.
    PS3570.R38M34 2013
    811'.54—dc23
                                        2012048409

To the memory of Julianna Mutti
who left this Earth before transforming it entirely
into her vision of liberty and justice for all.

There is no way out of the spiritual battle
the war is the war against the imagination
you can't sign up as a conscientious objector

—*Diane DiPrima,* "Rant"

Hope is definitely NOT the same as optimism.
It's not the conviction that something will turn out well,
but the certainty that something makes sense,
regardless of how it turns out.

—*Vaclav Havel,* "Hope"

TABLE OF CONTENTS

PREFACE

ON AVENIDA DE INSURGENTES SUR in Mexico City a billboard stands, advertising the Polyforum with its permanent exhibit, *The March of Humanity on Earth and Toward the Cosmos.* Under the word SIQUEIROS, there's a portrait of him wearing a crown of thorns made of bayonets. Like tin cans cut by shears into little churches, the graphic is typical of how Mexican folk-art can hook a passer-by's interest through visual metaphor. Triggered by that image, this book is an imagined voyage into four crucial years in the life of an extraordinary painter, Mexican Muralist José de Jesús "David" Alfaro Siqueiros, a life dedicated to experimental art and general rebellion.

He was born December 29, 1896 and died January 6, 1974. His mother died when he was four. His father, Cipriano, placed him with his grandfather, Don Antonio, who raised him on his bull-breeding farm in Chihuahua. Cipriano was a lawyer for the *hacendados* who controlled Mexican plantations with a feudal grip on the Indians working the land. David saw instances of cruelty, torture and death inflicted on *campesinos.* He could never forget them because he carried Mexico's contradictions in his blood, nor could he forgive the system that made their lives hellish. He was committed not just to expose it in paintings that became metaphors for the psychological underpinnings of Mexico's internal conflicts, but to fight it, literally and physically.

His adolescence was spent fighting in art school for native Mexican teachers and in the Mexican Revolution. When the war ended in 1920 he had risen to the rank of *Capitán secondo.* Some praised his courage under fire; others couldn't decide if he were brave or crazy. He fought in Venustiano Carranza's Army of National Liberation against, ironically, both the Villistas in the north and Zapatistas in the south whose platform, "Land and Liberty," were what he himself wanted for the people. He traveled Mexico by troop train, passing through cities with cathedrals and temple ruins, imagining what ancient Mexico was like to those who walked among its brightly-painted pyramids illuminating the nature of their gods.

In 1919 he traveled to Europe with his first wife, Graciela "Gatchita" Amador, and studied, along with Diego Rivera, both the Italian Renaissance murals of men like Michelangelo and the modernist work of Cezanne. With that vision he approached his former comrades-in-arms, now running the new Mexican government. He dreamed of a modern Mexico resplendent with murals that covered the interior and exterior walls of public buildings, giving the illiterate visual images that could kindle pride in their cultural history. How could they refuse this eager young man who fought so bravely beside them? With the advocacy of José Vasconcelos, the Syndicate of Mexican Revolutionary Painters (including Diego Rivera and José Orozco) set out to transform the National Palace and other public buildings into celebrations of Mexican revolutionary spirit. Yet Mexico's political leaders regretted their decision when he attacked them in the pages of the art magazine, *El Machete,* as sell-outs to the same plutocratic families who had ruled Mexico since the Conquest.

Who was this complicated man, at once a fighter and an artist? The more I read of his biography the more I was amazed at his toughness, his determination to realize his visions despite huge obstacles, not the least of which, the art market in the United States which turned away from social realism to abstract expressionism. Like many in the 1930s he was a passionate anti-fascist willing to take up arms, willing to go to prison for the then-illegal act of organizing unions for teachers, public workers, and miners. During his years living with the tempestuous Blanca Luz, Siqueiros painted as if with a blowtorch instead of a brush. "Apathy is collaboration with oppression," he told the people he worked with in mural projects. His greater quarrel, though, was with frames, whether frames of reference or being "framed." This is not to say he did no easel art. But he always tried to overwhelm the "fourth wall," the invisible field of numbness, in himself and others, resulting from being turned into things.

Except for flash-forwards to his imprisonment in the early 1960s and to the opening of "The March of Humanity," the poems here find Siqueiros in the years between 1936 and 1940, braiding his love for Angelica Arenal, his insightful visions into modern spiritual duress, and his antipathy toward Leon Trotsky, culminating in the attack on Trotsky's house. Following that, he flew to avoid prosecution under a Chilean visa written by Pablo Neruda.

Magician's Hat explores a verbal parallel to his mural style, a *concrete expressionism* or *social surrealism* where human figures and symbols gather into events, as opposed to the abstract expressionism and easel painting that were prevalent during his lifetime. His politics and his life are woven from his sensibilities and experience. The post-traumatic intensity and repetition of motif in his work runs counter to the usual aesthetic demand that each work be an autonomous statement. He paints metaphors for the human condition that evolved toward "The March of Humanity," where the beauty and inherent dignity of the human spirit emerges from the heart when it aspires to freedom, like what Albert Camus writes about in *The Rebel*, i.e. the discovery of what humanity rebels "in the name of." This dignity belongs to the oppressed and the oppressor. Even the rich who seem so in control are enslaved by the machine they have created. *The March* marks a difference in his theme. It is this difference—and whether the seeds of this difference may be seen in him prior to *The March*—that I became fascinated with.

At his death Siqueiros left the paintings and the enigma of a man who spent many years at war in Mexico and Spain as well as various stints in prison, years he could have been painting. Yet he had a profound artistic effect on his generation. Not only did he pioneer the use of acrylics but the question of how architecture influences the angular perceptions of a moving viewer. Indeed, Siqueiros persuaded Rivera to get past his apprenticeship to Picasso's Cubism and toward painting Mexican subjects. Jackson Pollock was present in Siqueiros' art studio in New York when Siqueiros showed him how acrylics blended into rainbows by spray-painting from a step-ladder on butcher paper laid on the floor. This became "action painting."

Magician's Hat begins in George Gershwin's apartment. It's a party to celebrate the unveiling of David's portrait of Gershwin at Carnegie Hall. Angelica Arenal, the woman who will become his second wife, walks into the apartment. He is stunned to recognize in this beautiful woman one loop in the strands of his life circling back to propel him into a visionary future in which "the march of humanity" never ceases, for in each generation the struggle continues. What essentially has changed from his time to ours?

GEORGE'S APARTMENT

Halloween Night, 1936

David Siqueiros hunched over a piano
beside his friend George,
a swan in white tux
                    as women in gowns
like clouds of daffodils, and men in black-tie
tuxedos bloomed on polar-bear carpets,

magnified through cigarette smoke
coiled above silver fingernails
                    sharp as chipped obsidian.

Art-deco bodies exhaled carbon atoms.
Sequined masks glinted asterisks. Pin curls
hooked around martini eyes.
                    Mirrors
on both walls cast pieces of him in infinite
recess and left him wondering what part

was still able to believe. When they leaned
back laughing he saw them as chrome
hood ornaments. They're only acting gay,

he told himself, pulling at his turtleneck.
It was déjà vu, only someone else's. He grinned.
—*They see me as the barbarian, no?*

—*Think of my guests,* George said, *as cash cows
        grazing in a white meadow giving green milk . . .*

David fished a cigarette from his pocket,
stared out the window, not at the pointillist maze of
Park Avenue apartment lights

                              but somewhere
he'd rather be, his Soho studio with Pollock's face
lighting up when he showed him how

spray-gunned Dupont car paint made rainbow
strings on studio floors, diaphanous clues
to the vanishing of Pollock's high school Eurydice.

                    Pollock's irises kaleidoscoped
with abstracts of his wind-tormented Texas.
a *barranca* filled with twisted tumbleweed,

                         lost in an anguish without cause,
without blame, leaving him a rage without object,
tearing his guts out with whiskey . . .

                    and into that room
stepped Angelica Arenal. David saw her turn
as the butler took her wrap, disclosing the tulip of

her strapless gown. Her tanned shoulders
sunset on Lake Chapala. He took in
the promising gravity of her bosom, the bow of

her brows, her lashes beating like oars on fateful voyages.
An aster bloomed in his chest and the night
                    no longer fit inside him.

George's hands were water-bugs on "It Ain't
Necessarily So."—*Your songs are on the lips of all Mexico,*
Angelica said. *Would you help President Cardenas*

fund his land reforms for the poor peasants?
George flung off the easel shroud. Voila!
                    Applause, applause.

Someone asked Siqueiros,—*Your work is,*
as they say, "engaged." How could you paint something so . . .
personal?—For the money.
               The crowd tittered.
Eye-to-eye Siqueiros leaned toward George's guest,
peered into the man's pupils until he reached a bottom

               that drew gasps. *Are you engaged with me?*
A woman asked if he thought they were vampires.
I don't know, he answered. *Show me your teeth.*

—*Da-vid!* George pleaded, *these are not the bad guys,*
turning the guests' attention to the painting,
Gershwin on-stage at the Steinway

in a packed Carnegie,
               three thousand rapt souls
imagining their immigrant parents as wind-blown

newspaper headlines swirling between skyscrapers,
rag merchants crying their wares, the whole
bluesy wonder of it. *Listen, folks . . .*

See that mug in the front row? That's Ira!
David's portrait is a family treasure.

But David wasn't listening. He and Angelica
were breathing the chemistry of each other's skin,
               pheromones of rich wet clay.

He jutted his chin to the exit. She nodded.
They turned for the door arm-in-arm.
He placed his hand lightly on the small of her back.

Ain't love grand? George gushed as they floated out,
dropping on elevator cables to 59th near Central Park
beneath crystal stars in a black liquid sky.

MAGICIAN'S HAT

Central Park South, minutes later

David and Angelica shushed through fallen leaves,
moving silhouettes against Essex Hotel lights.
Chauffeurs pulled up at liveried doormen
ushering top hats and mink stoles through revolving doors.
Valets skittered over sidewalks dusted with evening frost
hauling luggage through white clouds of exhaust.

David stopped to look at her again,
recognized a scrawny teen-ager years before
peeking at him from behind a bathroom door
as her mother rented him a room in East LA.

He got the neighborhood to take a hand in a mural.
He was painting a now to last, he told them
as he flashed sketches of a peasant crucified on
tangled vine branches beneath an eagle's wings.

They knew what the eagle was. Always there,
over their shoulder as they worked, ready to swoop.
Some only gave string, others labor days
erecting scaffolds or preparing brick to take fresco.

And after the unveiling on the restaurant rooftop,
a fiesta with old men ladling *chichirones* for children
hopping foot to foot impatient for steaming
sweet meat, fireworks, flags, dancing mariachis.

Now, in the just-falling snow of New York,
Siqueiros saw in Angelica's womanly face the girl

with the Brownie flash camera
who shook her fist at a truckload of *cabróns*
shot-gunning the mural, shouting "dirty
           commie red" as they careened past.

Siqueiros stood beside the horse of a hansom cab
peered in its eyes, saw oceans, galaxies.
—*I want,* he confided, *to make art inescapable*
    like two strangers falling in love.

—*Art,* she told him, *is a luxury I can't afford.*
She stroked the horse's oat-packed jaw.
How would he inspire her, she wanted to know.

He reached in his pockets for his touchstones,
three spent tubes of acrylic paint, his magician's hat.
—*From this I can make whatever world you wish,*
memories of your family lighting candles on gravestones
at midnight while dynamos throb golden in night skies.
he offered as he juggled them high in the air.

She saw his circus smile and smiled back.
—*What if it's not . . . ?*
—*Fine. Then I'll revise until it feels right.*

He leaned close to Angelica, his lips an inch
from hers, close enough to feel her heat.
Let's go to my studio and make a Titan.

She told him she couldn't, she was sailing at dawn
for Spain to cover the Civil War.
—*Then I'm going too . . . to look out for you.*

She pushed him away.—*A man will say he's*
protecting you, when he means to own you.

They saw men in ripped pin-stripe
suits and battered hats form a bread line
where two women handed out loaves.
Angelica wished she'd brought her camera.

Police vans lurched to a sidewalk stop.
A dozen cops jumped out, clicking nightsticks
on pavement, shoving the ragged men into paddy-wagons.

As the vans roared off with their meal of hunger,
he waved his fingers like a prestidigitator.
—*Let's give these gringos a run for their money.*
He hauled Angelica up on the cab, grabbed
the whip, cracked it over the horse's ear,
lurching toward Columbus Circle and the jail
        to harass the harassers in their lair.

ANGELICA'S LETTER FROM MADRID

19 February 1937

As is customary now, the bombardment began
at noon on a lovely day otherwise. I was on a trolley
coming back from the front, taking photos of General
Mola's African soldiers, (so strange to see their shining
faces in Spain). We were turning into the square when
I saw my hotel struck by artillery shells. An entire corner
of the fifth floor was blown to chunks of cement.

I ran into the lobby covered in gray dust.
Everybody was crouched under coffee tables. They
looked at me with mouths agape as if I were a ghost.
I couldn't help laughing, they looked so silly down
on the floor like that. And what does it matter how
my hair looks anymore?

The war has certainly affected me. I feel
my brain, my heart, every cell in my body has been
taken apart and made harder. I write this after
midnight by candle in the hotel basement near the
makeshift beds of the many new orphans. There's
a five-year-old with your eyes.

Before the madness I found a distant cousin.
Margarita, a nurse. Her hospital was the first building
Franco's forces hit. There's something cunning in
the fascist mind that knows how to encircle. to strangle
its enemy so it cannot heal its injuries and fight on.

I must go. A child has woken crying from
nightmares. And now they are all crying. They
need to be held. Impossible, but I try. They need
sterile bandages, disinfectant, surgical kits, any
kind of anesthesia, even aspirin.

I wish I could send you a photo so you could see. But there's no dark-room here. Ask George to donate to the Orphan's Relief Fund, which I am inventing. In fact, I don't want to see you unless you arrive in Madrid with medical supplies. I am entirely serious about this, *mi querido*.

WHAT HE RECALLS OF THE SPANISH CIVIL WAR

1 His First Assignment, Jarama River Valley, 1937

The station wagon taxiing him stopped.
He opened the door into howitzer rounds
       screaming through gray battlefield skies,
a chaos he knew too well. Thunderbolts.
       Gray smoke plumes
opened their wings and gathered men in.

       Still figures of two medics
jerked into motion, toting a man on a stretcher,
       a pink hole in his thigh.
He was propped on an elbow, smiling,
photographed by a war correspondent.
Down a dirt road, three light tanks clanked,
       tossing glops of muck.

His driver unloaded doors from bombed
Madrid apartments: yellow, blue, flamingo,
two-by-two straining against gravity to flap away
on hinges. Lives, families, shattered,
bathroom privacies exposed
       miles from this farm country.

Soldiers stacked ivory tusks, no, artillery shells,
tents, field hospitals, telephone poles.
A dust devil plucked at David' portfolio.
Hoisting his duffel, he crunched to the HQ bunker
handing his papers to General Gomez, swarmed by
lieutenants in shirt sleeves, by radio men
spilling the confetti of dispatches, desiderata of war.

Gomez asked David's military occupation.
—*Mexican revolution. Cavalry, artillery, Capitán secondo.*
A painter, also. He pulled out a poster of a tank called
"Liberdad" crushing tank-traps.
            To raise the men's morale.

Gomez needed a man to *command* a tank, not paint it,
gesturing with a tiny gold lighter, perfect for chigger
burning, with a wrist motion of slapping paint,
leading him by the patched elbow up a cratered hill
where yellow jackets, no, bullets, stung,
            issuing his order to reinforce trenches.

Rainbow doors got hammered in
to clouds of dirt, no, entrances to Hades.
Gomez handed David field glasses magnifying
another hill a mile away crawling with men.
—*Not only must we fight the fascists,*
Gomez harrumphed, *but Trotsky's vultures wait*
hoping to swoop in and snatch our victory.

He pointed toward the Jarama River bridge,
men in foxholes, green oranges in farther orchards,
            dusted with pastel green chalk.
A mile down the road, a tank from the Great War
chuffed before infantry in soft brown hats
sucking exhaust.—*Someone's got to warn Lt. Modesto.*
The General scribbled in his notebook,
ripping off a page. *That would be you.*

2 HIS HEART TANGOS WITH HIS THROAT

it's not a question of fear
between Madrid and unplowed farmlands
or bowing to whatever stars decree
one stone bridge with low Roman arches

shrapnel wounds from his first marriage to Gatchita
down into the black river Jarama
all that water gone under with Blanca Luz
crouching through orange tree boughs,
taking green globes in hand, sniffing them,
careful not to knock them off their stems
smile at the skull and the skull smiles back
the long scream of artillery from beyond
a man like a shell making one white funereal plume

He jogged past foxholes, asking for Modesto.
Men wearing the denims they enlisted in
jammed thumbs toward a pencil-thin moustache.
Siqueiros handed him the General's scribble.
—*Know anything about mortars?* the lieutenant asked.
—*It's too late for anything but dead reckoning.*

Modesto strapped in a .30 caliber belt.
Siqueiros zigzagged across the bridge, a sniper's
shots ricocheting like chipped flints.
The Lieutenant yelled,—*Are you the painter?*
—*Only when I'm painting!* David shouted back.

By intuitive parabolic trigonometry
his hands turned elevation screws. Men dropped
shells down tubes that bumped, arced and krumped
near advancing infantry.
⁣   To avoid a mortar hit
the tank lumbered off the road into orchards so thick
its barrel hit against tree trunks, couldn't fire on
bridge positions. He re-adjusted screws, another round
flashed, oranges
⁣   flew like pool balls on the break.

Anti-tank gun in hand, he somehow knew
the fat man with dusty spectacles squinting at him
was named Pedro. *You're going to load this,*
he told him, *and I'll aim and shoot.*

They got in range, knelt.
Their shell streaked phosphorous, blowing the tank
turret off, infantry men blown back, in retreat,
uniforms on fire.

      Pedro kissed the sky. From foxholes
men swarmed Siqueiros, lifted him on their shoulders.

3 You're In the Army Now

On a stack of pallets stepping up
in his Colonel's uniform a brown sea of men
slouched before him. He turned to Modesto,
who blew his whistle:—*Fall in!* The great unshaven
beast grumbled.

      Modesto showed them to "dress ranks."
—*You shouldn't expect much,* Pedro said. *We're anarchists.*
—*Without discipline you won't last a day,* David shouted,
Franco will gloat over your useless corpses.
He pulled his pistol, fired once at a cloud.
In the silence following, a locust buzz of bolts
chambered shells. All pointed their rifles at him.
—*We have you out-gunned,* Pedro grinned.
David smiled back at Pedro, holstering his Colt.
      —*Outgunned, "sir."*

Men laughed. Rifles lowered. Modesto demonstrated
the salute, fist to temple like dehorned bulls.
All but an anarchistic few.

4 An Artillery Barrage Climbs Suicide Hill

Two rows of dirt-black rose bushes
burst out of the ground. Sweaty faces twitched.
Pedro shouted,—*A dance of death!*
He tried to scramble out. Siqueiros yanked him back.

Why are we always outgunned? Pedro asked.
—*Because fascists always have more money.*
—*Yes, yes, but why is that?*
—*Because that's all they are,* Siqueiros tapped
Pedro's chest, *while we must be something more.*
The long ripping whine of a cannon shell . . . BOOM
carbide smoke, men flying into trench walls,
blackness . . .

5 KNOCKED UNCONSCIOUS, SIQUEIROS DREAMS HE'S A BOY IN CHIHUAHUA

. . . the smell of hot lather on horses' necks
rasped his nostrils. He was flying alongside the buggy
until his grandfather Don Antonio pulled it to a stop
      at a big hacienda's veranda steps.

Campesinos ringed a young man lashed to a post
with sisal rope, his naked back a grill-worked canvas
where welts filled with blood.
      with claw-marks of feudal law,
with canticles of castigation.

Don Antonio's young wife, Eusebia, sat beside him,
rocking like an asylum inmate, not looking at
Don Reynaldo Arellano, the *hacendado*
on his Guadalajara cane chair with cobra hood
supervising his foreman as he lashed his victim.

Peons flinched at every stripe.
The dreamer reached through purple bougainvillea shade,
puzzled at why his hand was a small boy's,
tugging his grandfather's sleeve to make it stop.

Through the crowd another boy walked.

13

jammed the foreman's spine with a rusty pistol.
The foreman spun, slapped the kid so hard
        he went flying in dust.
Finally Don Antonio spoke.—*For this you ask us here?*

Don Reynaldo flicked his Cuban.
—*What can I do,* he shrugged. *The wretch defies me.*
With his cigar he prompted his foreman
to give the youth another stripe for good measure.
The foreman pulled the young man's head back.
Even his hair was unconscious.
—*This is not the dark ages!* Don Antonio bellowed.

—*Kill me, too!* the peasant boy cried out.
If you don't, some day I'll kill you . . . and everyone like you!
The foreman stepped toward him, whip arm raised.
Don Reynaldo shouted: *Silence, Pancho!*
       or you'll end up like your brother.
               The foreman cocked his arm . . .

a dozen doves lit on orange roof-tiles.
The crowd held its breath. David flew down
off the buggy to Pancho, covered him with his body,
and saw the last light of the young man's life
drain from his eyes. The foreman's arm

hung in the air. The *hacendado* asked Don Antonio.
       —*Who is this boy?*
—*The son of two great houses, and if you lay a finger on him . . .*
Arellano jumped up, turned to enter his house.
—*Don't threaten me, old man!*

Peasant women freed the young man's wrists,
covered his body with dusty rebozos. Four vaqueros
lifted him by his armpits, ghosted his corpse toward
the huts, the foreman among them.
None turned an angry eye on him.

David heard a woman mutter.
—*The Foreman must do as the owner says . . .*
the owner must do as the North Americans say.
Above, an eagle tilted its wings in the wind.
Don Antonio yelled at the lord as he exited.
—*One day the peasants will explode like a bloody volcano!*
In passing, the foreman lightly touched David's
        cheek with his whip . . .

6 WITH A FACE TICKLE

     . . . Siqueiros startled up
from the dream of his dream, scratched the itch,
heard artillerymen sneeze dirt. A salvo slammed
behind them, formed a cobra of smoke. He brushed
dirt out of his hair, hoisted himself up from the grave.

—*Do you want to die?* Pedro asked after
waiting a long time to see if his leader were dead.
—*I spit in death's face,* Siqueiros smiled. *It's a Mexican thing.*
He pulled out his wallet, unfolding
a drawing of a woman with arms like Athena's,
with solacing breasts and straight-on eyes
that would give a man everything in her soul,
        her skin white as a Castilian rose.
She's why I'll survive this . . . now
let's dig out of this mess and return fire on Franco.
—*It was Trotsky,* Pedro told him.
—*Trotsky? I thought his battalion didn't have artillery.*
—*They got some from somewhere. Maybe from here.*

Pedro pulled out a newspaper clipping,
a photo of a man with glasses, white goatee
caught mid-stride walking down a gangplank.
"Mexican President grants asylum to exiled Russian

revolutionary, Leon Trotsky," read the caption.

The men barked as they dug themselves out.
—*We follow you out of respect for the Mexican Revolution.*
But has Mexico gone nuts? Trotsky's a traitor!

Siqueiros recognized Frida in the photo.
What was she doing in Trotsky's company?
He promised his men the Judas would be
driven from Mexico
        if he had to do it himself.

A SQUARE IN VALENCIA

A lorry lumbered through rubble lanes.
From under tarp, men's voices sang:

> *There's a valley in Spain called Jarama.*
> *It's a place that we all know so well,*
> *for 'tis there that we wasted our manhood*
> *and most of our old age as well.*

Truck brakes gasped to a stop.
Shops, second-story flats, a bombed out library
chunks of broken concrete, steel beams twisted like straw.
Book pages riffled in the back draft.
Modesto and David jumped down.
Others met wives, mothers, smile-kissing chatter.

Through the crowd a five-year-old girl
piggy-backed her baby sister in a winding-sheet sling
        faces caked in dust, eyes
darting, expecting bullets, skies full of black crucifixes.

The older girl held out her hand
passing among people who drifted away
like battlefield smoke.
        Siqueiros pulled colored pencils
from his map case, sat on ruined church steps
sketching the child-mother. Line by stroke,
Modesto watched the portrait appear
out of nothing. The older sister carried the baby
as she was taught by her mother before
bombs blew her to pink mist . . .
two starved girls, molded by twilight,

hair streaked with war dirt, the baby's nose,
cheeks, brown eyes snapped to a net-bag of oranges,
set down by a mother hugging her son.

The girl had a rent in her shirt
the shape of a red chili. She sidled barefoot
toward the oranges, hoping.

All that was left, infinitely shredded nerves,
bellies swollen, brick-red cheeks and behind them
Siqueiros heard from thirty years before
girls holding hands singing

> *The patio of my house is very particular*
> *it's wet or dry like any other*
> *There the pretty girls crouch and stoop*
> *and the first one to sit is the winner . . .*

The girls gave each other an over-the-shoulder glance,
carrier and carried. David sketched ghosts of two
copper-red horse spirits who guided them and were them.
The older girl inched, stood point-blank,
close enough to peek into his map-case
for anything to eat. He held out a ripe orange,
          the treasure of Valencia.
She dragged her right foot as she walked away,
her sister the hunch on her back.

HOTEL VALENCIA

Under dining-room candelabras
with magnifying glass Angelica proofed
photos of dead partisans, gray faces
strewn crazy-quilt like trash in ditches,
machine-gunned by supposed allies.
—*Dispatches from the front?*
She glanced up.—*You said you'd look out for me.*
David smiled.—*War can be such a distraction.*

They rose in a rococo iron elevator,
opened a room. Moonlight streamed into
their broken marriages, raked by searchlights.
Then the dance of fevered undressing,
her cameras thudded, his map case split open.
They collapsed on the bed, a tangle of limbs.
He undid her hair. An obsidian waterfall
        splashed on her bare shoulders.

Their bodies locked, rocking.
The drone of bombers, ack-ack pulsing spondees.
Siqueiros saw flashes mirrored in Angelica's eyes.
two railroad lanterns swung by a soldadera
leaning off a caboose outside Cuernavaca,
bandolier strapped across her chest,
gasping at the clench of orgasm.
She found herself pushing dead bodies off her chest,
no screams, just heaving, opening her eyes.

Then, she, gathering sheets into a robe
got up, searching along the floor for cameras
to capture swastikas painted on wings, the proof.
Siqueiros rolled on the bed, reaching for her,
saw her hold his sketch,
        the two girls lit by

magnesium-white tracers, eyes like verbs,
sparking, dumping out her handbag,
a photo of her daughter, a blond girl, maybe six.
She told him she got it about his art, how
he made her stomach ache for the girls.
—*In war the little ones suffer most . . .*
But what's this, in the picture? Horses?

His interiors were filled with
whimsical horses, on paper, clouds on water,
souls from strewn bodies, leaves only sibyls could read.
His color palette was mixed with love and mourning,
with fists and kisses and dry eyes.
—*I'm only good at one thing, painting and fighting.*
—*That's two things.*

They kissed like drunken poets singing
on a Madrid rooftop, poets who promise to bring
each other in the small things of life
peace enough to go on with the struggle,
as if war were fireworks and only
spilled wine covered the cobblestone streets.

WEDDING

David and Angelica skipped up stairs
not cathedral marble but in the Mayor's
office the double window crystal
where light winked like a cobalt lighthouse,
the banks of bowed secretaries at typewriters
clacking like an industrial piano concerto.

David and Angelica faced each other,
Modesto, Ernesto, best men, the Mayor
in tuxedo, top hat, red sash, asked for the ring.
Siqueiros produced a golden butterfly necklace.
Clicking its clasp into place around her neck
he vowed.—*We will travel the immense road of life*
so close that with each step we will go forward,
together, bringing about the world we seek.

The Mayor cleared his throat.
—*By the power rooted in me by Spain,*
        such as it is, you are joined.
The couple kissed to general applause,
ran down the staircase out the door,
then passed under officers' crossed swords
toward a green staff car. Angelica threw
her bouquet. Pedro caught it.
A soldier crooned,—*O, Pedro, marry me!*
Pedro blusters in walrus: *I . . . I don't believe in marriage.*
I'm an anarchist. I believe in . . . free love!

CAFE BARCELONA

May Day, 1937

Suspended from gray cornices
striped awnings like Bedouin tents
cast shade on stone sidewalks.
Siqueiros, Modesto, and Ernesto Hemingway
sprawled at a café table hearing, down street, classical guitars,
       splashing fountains,
a hundred miles from artillery hammerings.

He would have liked to sketch this haven,
to thicken the air around the tables,
to limn the slouch of the waiter, tray under arm,
cocked against the doorway, cigarette in lips,
a slant of evening light across his face
revealing his daydreams in its chiaroscuro.

Three glasses clinked,
Ernesto offered a seventh toast,
full ash trays spilled out over the table.
David tossed his down.—*I've swallowed a bad star.*

—*How long's it been since Angelica . . . ?*
Ernesto bit his tongue. Bad form to mention
Siqueiros' heart-ache. The waiter set another round,
Modesto knew Angelica sailed to her mother's sick-bed.
Strong women are impossible, but who cares about the other kind?
Ernesto said, changing the subject, flicking his cigar.
Modesto raised his glass.
—*May this limpid fire extinguish the flames of your sweet Hell.*
Ernesto raised his glass.—*Here's to knowing how it ends!*
They dropped a few bills on the table,
stumbled, leaning, slightly tipsy, on one another,
three camels scuffling sand, the reins dangling down
as evening came on . . .

gunfire!
The high heels of a woman clacking over cobblestone.
The three sprinted to a pile of dead horses.
In a plaza they saw a brigade charge on foot,
red banners bent toward P.O.U.M. HQ
with machine pistols, grenades.
—*What is this?* Ernesto asked.
—*Trotsky,* a fallen soldier moaned.

As he pressed a kerchief to the soldier's wound
Siqueiros growled,—*Again? Will I ever be rid of him?*
The man's soul rushed invisibly out of his mouth.

—*He's taken death for an aspirin,* Ernesto sighed.
A cloud burst. The streets filled with rain.
Siqueiros picked up the dead man's trench coat
covering his head as he grabbed a machine-pistol.

—*Toss me that clip.* He caught it, clicked it in.
fired a shot from the horsemeat barricade.
—*Do you believe in an afterlife?* Ernesto asked.
—*You mean, do I have friends in high places?*
Ernesto nodded as he sighted along his barrel.
Maybe one, Siqueiros answered, wondering how
he would paint the form, the function, of another
armed man walking on a lagoon of blood.

LAZARO CARDENAS' OFFICE

Winter, 1940

At Lazaro's plush purple drapes
Siqueiros stood in his officer's uniform,
newspaper in armpit, watching traffic circle.
He saw, across Constitution Plaza, men, women,
stepping onto government building balconies to view
hundreds below, carrying *luminarios* single-file,
                    spelling the Virgin's outline
like flaming ink from a pen, glittering
on the Archbishop's gold embroidered robe.

Through car engine back-firing like snipers
a tour-guide's voice through bullhorn:

> —*The soil you stand on was once a lake bed*
> *piled layer by layer from primordial ooze*
> *into the city called Tenochtitlan, the Aztec*
> *capital which the Conquistadors discovered . . .*

—Dis . . . covered? Siqueiros choked.
Why do you permit these outrageous lies, Lazaro?
—*Alas, we need the tourist dollars,* Lazaro sighed,
then changed the subject.—*Do you have a wall to paint?*
—*Yes. In the electricians' union building.*
—*Ah, well. Get your money up front.*
Siqueiros unfurled the newspaper, the headline:

TROTSKY PLOTS STALIN'S DEATH

> —*Beneath these stones lie ruins of an ancient temple*
> *built to honor their war god, Huitchlipochli.*
When Siqueiros mentioned the rumor
that Lazaro supplied Trotsky with howitzers in Spain,
Lazaro shouted his denial, shouted his denial

that Trotsky was anti-Soviet, anti-revolutionary.
—*Ah, I've touhed a nerve,* David snapped.

Lazaro reached for a cigar to calm himself.
David kicked the Presidential desk.
Cardenas bent a goose neck lamp to assess damage,
then turned his Cuban, lighting it evenly.
—*We were comrades in the revolution*
and I honor that. But you can't talk to me that way.
      I'm President of Mexico.

      —*Today the descendents of the Aztecs*
      dance to honor their proud heritage.
      The dancers will allow you to photograph them
         for a small gratuity.

Lazaro told David through billows that Stalin
hatched plots against his regime. David asked why
Lazaro couldn't see through Trotsky's slander.
—*The Colonel hauled in one of his spies,* Lazaro offered,
and after some 'inducement' he told us everything.

      —*The cathedral you see before you*
      was built from stones taken from the Aztec temple.
      where savage priests tore the hearts from human
      sacrifices to their cruel gods.

Lazaro held his cigar at arm's length as he said
I'm puzzled by your loyalty to Stalin. Everybody but you knows
he's a psychopathic murderer. Why don't you wise up?
Or are you still carrying the cross for your father?
—*Keep my family out of this! My mistakes are my own.*
A better world. Isn't that what we fought for, Lazaro?

—*I fought for Mexico, not the world.*
As for Trotsky, the enemy of my enemy . . .
he showed me how to use union strikes to cripple

then nationalize Rockefeller's oil holdings in Tampico.
I've moved him to Diego and Frida's house, a virtual fortress.
Lazaro placed a comforting hand on David's shoulder.
Now we have PEMEX and Mexico will own its oil.
Don't bother yourself with such matters, David.
Be happy. Go paint your mural.

   —As we enter the cathedral please observe silence.
   The local people worship the sacred heart of Jesus
   with intense humility and devotion.

—You think painting is what, my hobby?
Lazaro tapped David on the chest: *If his death comes, it comes.*
But I will take it as a personal betrayal
   if it comes through you.
David brushed Cardenas' finger away,
grabbed his trench coat, stomped out of the office.
And take off that uniform! Lazaro yelled into David's wake.

MEETING ADRIANNA AT ANGELICA'S HOUSE

Siqueiros stood in portico shadows watching
Angelica read to the blond girl in the photograph
she had shown him by searchlight in Valencia.
Mother and daughter leaned together in slanted atrium light.
Was there room in his life for a child, he wondered.
The girl's hair caught fountain sparkles.
He heard Angelica's voice rise:
—The Devil told you that! shouted the little man.
And in his rage he stamped his foot so deep in the earth
he sank up to his waist. Then Rumplestilskin seized his left leg
with both hands . . . and tore himself in half!
The girl giggled at the imp's rage, then her eyes drifted.
—Who's that, mamma?
Angelica hugged her.*—My husband, baby.*
David walked over and picked up the child.
—How's my little princess?
She wriggled like a sunfish in his hands.
He smoothed back one of her tresses with his lightest touch.
Angelica took Adrianna back from his arms.
—David still believes in fairy-tales.
Adrianna smiled shyly at David.*—So do I.*
—Lupita! Angelica called.
The housekeeper stepped through the kitchen door.
Run along now, I want to talk grown-up. Angelica said,
tapping Adrianna's shoulder.
The girl skipped off, stopped, turned to wave.
David looked into Angelica's eyes.
Your father's in the hospital. Go say your goodbyes.
He touched the gold pin on her dress.

HOSPITAL

Night

A nursing nun drew back the curtain.
His father, boxed in a clear-plastic oxygen tent.
Tubes led to phlegm-clogged lungs.
The taste of incense in the room put Siqueiros
in a white Communion suit walking out of church
for the last time sickened by the stench of sanctimony.

David stepped up to this weathered piece of driftwood,
once a lion of the law, noting contract ink
on the old man's claws, drying under an electric lamp.
His father's lids opened like surprised lips:
—*You must be busy . . . with your . . . revolution and . . .*
The years in his father's face were cross-hatched lines
crushing in on themselves like caked mud.

He could count his father's fleshless ribs
under the hospital tissue he was wrapped in.
Perhaps now his nearness to death would help his father
see laborers plodding sidewalks, so exhausted
they can't lift their eyes to the haven of a mural.
I understand . . .
            business, not . . . politics . . .

—*My politics is what you might call
'audience development,'* David explained,
but his father's body convulsed so hard
the wedding portrait on his bed stand wobbled.
A slim frock-coated youth with moustache,
Siqueiros' white-veiled mother standing
far away enough to be an arranged bride.

His father's hand placed a silver crucifix in his:
—*You were always . . . a saint abroad . . . and a devil . . . at home . . .*

28

When your mother died, I . . .
Siqueiros held the cross up to the lamp beside the screen
and there in tableaux an apparition of Cuauhtémoc
tortured by Cortés for the location of the gold,
drooled over by the leashed dog of war
in its iridescent armor
                    even as his father
coughed out his final fear of not enough money
for a proper tomb that seized his chest his whole life.
I left you . . . with your grandfather . . . it's not good . . .
for a boy . . . to grow up . . . with a father . . .
who can't stop . . . grieving . . .
Siquerios' gaze traveled to Malinche.
He read the lips of her two cubist faces.
                    Cortés, pones la llama a sus pies.
Waves of flame consumed the Aztec's feet.
—*I stopped grieving when I was five,* Siqueiros
held the crucifix to his father's lips.
A silver light beamed from Cipriano's hair.
Your grandfather . . . he could laugh . . . at God's jokes . . .
                    married a woman . . . half his age . . .
I'm . . . I'm . . . he rasped faster, faster.
The uncertain light filled the room, filled Siqueiros.
He ran into the corridor.—*Help! A man is dying here!*

DREAM OF THE PERMANENT INWARD GAZE

Fair-weather clouds float gulf-ward
through a sepia sky
        face-up over the *zócalo*
like sea otters on gentle waves.

Government buildings form a squared U
opened to cathedral spires splinted in bamboo scaffolds.
The people's space is covered in an anodyne of frost
        like a Mexican Bruegel
that numbs the sleeper, bound on the wheel,
his eyes an offering to the ravens.

Breezes furl a huge silk Nazi flag half-mast,
luffing above pavement scarred with wheel ruts
where Aztec slaves hauled temple stone
and where an artist has set up his easel.

Nothing of the artist can be seen
but his paint-flecked hands adding small
strokes to a peasant woman's portrait.
She kneels over a dead child, her fingers
a mud rake at redemption's shuttered gates.
Two boys lean, one on each of her shoulders.
Her head is covered by a woven *rebozo*.
A voice from the sky says,
This woman has the four-hundred year inward gaze.

A slim, white-haired man, silver beard,
stops to view the painting. He carries a dozen
calla lilies, pulls one, splits its stalk with his thumbnail,
smears the painting with the sap so hard it
clatters to the pavement, covered with centuries of worn
shoe leather, dried spit and humiliation.

He beckons the invisible painter with crooked finger
to follow him into the cathedral,
SANTA THERESA carved on its lintel.
His heels clack as he plods on cobblestone.
The sky coughs as he enters the cathedral's black mouth.
On the walls, painted in concrete expressionism,
are scenes from the Via Dolorosa,

       Roman whips and thorns.

A heavy-set bruiser in sunglasses comes out,
tapping with a stick toward the empty easel.
Through fish-eye lenses his gold fillings smile
like votive candle cups. and behind him

       twin cathedral towers
with stained-glass windows depicting smoky

       blue gargoyles, twitching in fits.
He hears among sputtering torches, insect stritches,
a *campesino*'s last *centavo* clinking in the poor box . . .

       a women's long wail.
The dreamer's blind hand sliding along the stone wall.
finding a spot, an invisible opening

       where his fingers disappear . . .

PANIC BREATHING

Siqueiros jolted up in bed,
eyes twin lakes emptying down his cheeks.
He mistook Angelica's sheer nightgown
for his father's cerements. She drew a breath,
her breasts rose. She held the air in
paranormal vacuum hush, then released it.

He watched his sleeping woman breathe,
reaching behind him to fumble a cigarette
out of a pack. He lit it and laid back
against the headboard forming a triangle
like a smoking volcano. What fire would he not
rain upon the world if he should lose her?

She woke.—*What's troubling you?*
—*It was my father. I asked what he wanted.*
He wouldn't say. Angelica held him.
—*Sometimes the dead play charades.*
He told her "Theresa" was carved
on the cathedral door.—*Your mother's name,*
she noted, snapping on the night light,
startled by a new painting
            on an easel of a man naked
from the waist up, head encased in mud,
hands pleading.
            Do you ever sleep?
He could not sleep or else he dreamed.

He got up and padded to the bathroom.
Angelica raised her voice so he could hear.
The man in your painting has no eyes.
Her voice sounded like she was underwater.

He splashed his face, looked in the mirror,
his eyes a lightless closet of souls, his mouth

leaking smoke like the god Tezcatlipoca
        making him see his secret fears.
His face was the no-face in the painting
covered in clay as thick as his not wanting to hear
the cacophony of political lies that made him ill.
He wanted no ears for the trump of doom.
No eyes for Mexico, bought and sold by investment banks.
No nose to smell the corruption.
No mouth to announce the day's arrival
when the legal thievery is too huge,
when there are so many children starving
one cannot feed them all or lie down
with the lepers of austerity and give them love,
the lies so outrageous people go into shock
stepping on their own tongues, stunned by
the spectacle of men too powerful to bring to trial.
What else is to be done but stand with hands
outstretched, pleading,
        head encased in mud?
—*Does it have a title?*

—*I . . . call it . . . "Our Cur . . . rent Image,"* he stammered.
He couldn't bear to look. What if he'd been wrong?
He looked instead at his white-knuckled hands
strangling a towel so hard his forearms shook.
He wished he had a pure blue canvas
        the color of the Virgin's robe.
The sink hollowed his voice as he asked her
what the chances were she could post an article.

It's getting harder, she answered. *Nobody wants to hear it.*
But Contreras wants to ask you how old you were
        when you first read Marx.
Lightning made wet garden palmettos
visible for a second through the windows.
The leaves cut him, bled ink on his neglected memoirs.
He had to set the record straight.

He pulled on paint-speckled pants, asked her
to fish out pen and paper, take notes.
Angelica moaned.—*I'm not your slave.*
I need my sleep if I'm going to get through tomorrow.

—*It's already tomorrow. We can sleep when the struggle is over.*
—*I'm as committed as you!*
She stumbled out of bed, crossed to her dressing table,
took out a pen. *OK, what do you want me to write?*
—*Write: People ask me when I first read Marx.*
My answer is, I didn't get my politics from a book.
Angelica scribbled, then paused, head on forearm.
—*Why do you want me to write this?*
What is this, a self-justification? You don't . . .
—*No. Look, it's a record. Let others judge, if they must.*
—*Here. You write it.* Angelica handed him the pen,
staggered over to the bed and flopped on it.
David took the pen in hand, wrote:

> *1910. Pancho and I sat on the corral fence.*
> *Don Antonio's trainer worked the young bull*
> *with cape and sword, observing whether he led*
> *with right or left horn. Clouds erased our shadows*
> *on the arena floor. Pancho said he was sorry*
> *my grandfather died. I was sorry about his brother*
> *whipped to death by Don Reynaldo Arellano.*
> *Pancho said he'd remember his brother when he ended up*
> *in some skirmish in the revolution already started*
> *by the brothers Flores-Magón in Baja,*
> *dead with his tail tossed to a senorita by some elegant*
> *killer in a pinche spangled suit and puta shoes.*
> *We heard the chug-chug sputter of a Stanley*
> *Steamer approaching Don Antonio's hacienda.*
> *I told him the trick to survival is always to be*
> *unpredictable. And to know which side you're on,*
> *he added. I'm on your side, I told him. He asked*
> *who's that rich man in the car? My father, I confessed.*

Come to take you home? I said my home no matter where I am, will always be with you.

CHAPULTEPEC PARK

Later that morning, with flashbacks to adolescence and Spanish Civil War

Paint-box clamped in armpit
Siqueiros dashed through Paseo traffic,
images from his dream still flashing in his mind.
The bus smoked off without him
to blacken the Angel of Independence.

Left on the sidewalk, he watched cloud flotillas
sail between heaven and the central plateau,
the sky's bowl like sea foam lit by sun disk.
From asphalt black streets skyscrapers rose
with pomegranate pink lines,
radio towers on jagged rooflines,
turning cranes moving to boulevard morning
rush hour traffic blur. the city's heart
the graph on which his brain scratched its dance.

He sat on a green bench,
catching his breath as a boy in red
jacket looked in his bloodshot eyes,
and, as if he'd heard the thunder of hell,
broke in panic from his father's grasp,
ran toward traffic.
           His father
yanked him back to the sidewalk . . .
a lit crystal candelabra hangs in Cipriano's drawing-room.
Don Reynaldo Arellano stands at a desk . . .
a fourteen-year-old David tries to snake by sliding oak doors . . .
his father invites him in to introduce his client,
unaware David has met the hacendado years before . . .
David runs out the door into the cobbled street . . .
throws a stone through his father's window . . .

His veins clenched each time pile-drivers
pounded girders deep to lake bottom
BOOM   BOOM   BOOM
his whole body jerked, *bombers drop incendiaries*
through his lungs, fires in his legs, the impulse to run,
to plow up the park shell-shocked, with his horns . . .

Angelica was right.
There was no explanation.
There was only the march of images in a dream,
a painted-stained pair of hands,
a cathedral door, a dead man still angry.

He turned to the boy, then pointed upward:
At the portals of the sky, he sang,
they sell shoes to the angels so they can walk upon the clouds . . .
The boy stopped sniffling and smiled.

THE COLONEL COMES CALLING

A black sedan, gleaming chrome grill
sidled   stopped   no din, just
the *zzz* of a right rear window sliding down,
a dead fish voice Siqueiros recognized
from the revolution. He bent in half to look inside.
Salazar in his Chief of State Police uniform.

David climbed into the Colonel's web on wheels.
—*To the Electricians' Union Building,* the uniform told his driver.
Siqueiros grinned.—*Is there anything you don't know about me?*
The unmarked Buick carved the rotary.
The Angel of Independence reached up,
holding the promissory note for heavenly rewards,
yet trapped by one toe in its terrestrial prison.

The Colonel offered a cigarette.—*Still interested in politics?*
He flamed both cigarettes with a gold lighter.
Siqueiros opened an ash tray in the door,
—*You've been ghosting me since I got back from Spain.*
The Colonel's eyebrow raised slightly.
—*Maybe you should have stayed there.*
Then you wouldn't be pursuing the fantasy
that your god-like artistic powers will free
      the poor-in-spirit from their gloom.

Banks flashed stock quotes in digits.
It's Friday, the clocks said.
Traders were taking profits from teachers' pensions,
from farmers' children, buying houses
they planned to burn to the ground.
They knew how to make money from disasters.
      They had bought insurance.

Hundreds of file clerks, all aluminum elbows,
knees, silver spiked high heels, black plastic

umbrella rapiers, crowded into skyscrapers,
the scythes of their mouths grim as they steeled
themselves to turn humans into "data."
—*Is this the change we fought for?*
The Colonel sneered.—*We fought for pocket change.*

Along the Paseo men in gray jump-suits
swept sidewalks with palmetto brooms between
busts of Mexico's heroes and royal palms.
—*The way the workers get screwed never changes.*
Siqueiros reached, took the Colonel's
sunglasses off, startled to see an eight-year-old
in military costume, epaulets, medals, hat dwarfing him.
His brushy eyebrows looked glued on.
Siqueiros fought back a smile as he watched
the boy Salazar lift his cigarette to his little mouth.
—*Please, no rants,* he squeaked.
Just don't go to the march against Trotsky.

Sun sliced his eyes through the still-opened window.
—*What march?*
—*Don't play stupid, David.*
The Colonel put his sunglasses back on.
Siqueiros saw reflected in the Colonel's mirrors
himself as a young Captain on a troop train
with machine-guns chugging north to Sonora.
1919. Locomotive steam, Cigarette smoke.
The Mexican time-machine.
Monte Alban's stone gods. Oaxaca's church spires.

Sunlight glittered on the Colonel's medals, epaulets.
—*Let me paint your portrait. You're ready now.*

At the corner of Insurgentes a traffic cop
in leather jacket, jodhpurs, white helmet, wrote
a ticket with quetzal pen on a white-haired cabbie,
who, hands together, prayed, fervent to be let off.

—*A pitiful sight, a man with no palanca,* the Colonel observed.
But as a hero of the revolution you could write your own ticket
          if you'd just …
—*That's exactly what I must not do, Leandro.*

The car slowed to a red light stop.
Beggar women held their babies in their arms.
David quick opened the Colonel's door, jumped out,
and, as a *collectivo* swung by, jumped on,
flipping his cigarette out that hit
the Buick's windshield in a disaster of sparks.

ELECTRICIANS' UNION BUILDING

Curved twin staircases drew the eye up
to the mural's steel power stanchions painted
on the ceiling, leaning their tips toward the sun disk
with white sails of electric plasma,
while on one side the hawk-beaked minister of Finance
sent the temple of Justice up in flames,
and on the other side. death pointing its rifle
quite nakedly at the endless ranks of human beings
fed by gas-masked spooks into the foreground
the painting's point. Looked at from above
the whole assemblage was absurd. Why would
human beings allow themselves to be herded
by a few armed soldiers toward the minting press
       that stamps them into coins
as if Midas had at last learned not to mind
when his touch turned his children to gold
splashing out to the occult beneficiaries,

they who make and burst bubbles,
they who receive the sun's bounty transmuted
by coal-fired dynamos into lightning waves
by men and lizards in Vulcan's caves,
they whose commandments speak from
radio tower factory smokestacks
where the automaton, made animate, eats all,
rich and poor, stokers of flame, the whole inferno,
top, sides, bottom engulfing the viewer inside
life's history,
       from its out-gassing springs
to amoeba to lungfish to humankind —
nothing left but pools of sludge, a bleak vision
except the greater crime would be to turn away,
to flee into the babble of doubt, quibbling over minutia,
or some tale where water kills the witch,
for how is the enormity of it to be conceived,

this enormous magic machine that convinces
every man and woman they must work for it
at a wage that kills the soul or the body will die?

Luis heard Siqueiros' footsteps on marble.
His waggling cigar stub chided his friend for being late
as he clambered up the platform's bamboo triangles.
—*Salazar picked me up again,* Siqueiros grumbled,
swooping up his spray-gun, connecting hose,
flipping on switch, forming silvery black eagle
swept-back bomber wings hovering over its
                    panicked prey, easy pickings.

Luis chewed his stub, hang-dog that David
promised him the eagle but reneged, obsessed
with fashioning one with iron feathers that
can slice flesh, claws that made Mexico
                    a bandit-ridden hell-hole.

Luis asked when he was going to have a say.
—*Who's the maestro here?* Siqueiros barked.
Luis took his cigar out of his mouth.
—*I looked for you at the farm collective meeting
last night in Xochimilco. Where were you?*

A beggar-woman with crying infant
padded into the hall, looked at the mural,
spat on tiled floor, breast-feeding.
It's impolite to stare, Luis said.
—*Years ago I challenged Diego to paint a beggar-woman.
He picked up a charcoal and found her curves.
The muralist movement was born in that moment.*
The baby stopped crying.
Siquieros wondered how to paint her feeding Mexico.
Luis's voice climbed into the sound vacuum.
—*The Bank of Commerce is foreclosing on them.*

What David felt at others' woe
pulled apart the web he used to trap his rage.
He slammed the spray-gun down, tore his apron off,
rushed out, past tourist junk shops,
alleys of homeless living off restaurant garbage.
Picking up a loose sidewalk brick he entered
the Bank of Commerce, leaned over a dowager.
—*How can you put your money in a bank that forecloses*
on poor farmers who've tilled the same soil five hundred years?
The woman looked up at him.—*Don't hurt me!*
Two bank guards rushed over:—*He's got a brick!*
A flash: guns at his head on marbled floor.

MAKING BAIL

Clanging jail cell doors triggered
the *déjà vu*. Thrown up against his old
friends, the brick wall graffiti, Siqueiros
lounged on the usual stained bunk.
It was 1926 again, arrested for organizing
a miner's union. He checked crude drawings.
—*Not bad*, he joked to his cell mates
who turned their backs, caught entirely
        without a sense of humor.

Solid hours began flaking apart
from cell bar to rusted stool, his stomach's fist
tight like waiting for his mother
and the new baby near the carriage barn
where he drew in the dirt with a stick
making dry creeks he thought of as writing,
then giggled. In the hour's vacuum
he imagined more obsessively than ever.

A mustachioed guard curled his finger.
Siqueiros gestured to his chest.
—*Yes, you,* the guard said.
Beyond the cage a heavy-set man in sunglasses
sporting a silver-handled cane smiled at him,
        too familiar, over his shoulder.

Out on the street it was night,
the air filled with a strangeness that
blistered his view of houses and shops.
In a cafe down street from El Pocito
this not-quite-stranger handed Siqueiros his card:
        MANUEL SUAREZ Y SUAREZ
           ENTREPENEUR
—*I've got a job for you.*
—*I don't want a job.*

—Why not?
—A job is a life sentence.
—How will you live?
—Like the birds of the air.
Suarez y Suarez lit two cigarettes, gave David one.
—I'm building a grand hotel, the biggest in the world
here in Mexico

        and I want you to paint the lobby.
Siqueiros had met this man's like in Buenos Aires,
New York, Paris, Rome, a face like graph paper.
—You got the wrong guy. I'm an artist, not a decorator.
Suarez y Suarez snapped his fingers.
—And I'm a rich man who gets what he wants.
A waiter appeared, bent, his ear at Suarez's mouth.
—You wouldn't like what I'd paint.
Tourists don't want their nice day spoiled.
—They see beggars in the streets, and go home glad to know
how much better off they are. It's the tourist experience.
The waiter placed two tequilas on the table,

        parabolic lime quarters.
Sprinkling salt on his thumb web, licking it,
Surarez held up his shot glass, saluted Siqueiros,
then threw the liquid down.
—Why sacrifice your art to politics?
As a hero of the Revolution you could write your own ticket.

        Perhaps I could induce you . . .
Siqueiros blunted out his cigarette
on his calloused hand, hoping the pain
would vault him out of this nightmare
with the President, the Colonel
and now the businessman

        talking from the same script.
—Others have tried.
—But that was only your life. I could make
one phone call and funding your art would not be

        in the national interest.

—*Very subtle.* David said, standing up,
his chair sprawled behind him, steaming off.
Suarez shouted as Siqueiros got further away.
—*You're so judgmental, David. I'm not Satan.*
You think I've been rich all my life? No.
I came here from Spain with less than nothing.
I have many wounds from fighting in the revolution.

Siqueiros stopped, turned back.
—*Where were you wounded?*
—*I was a traveling salesman in the grain business*
when I was captured by Villa's men.
They were going to execute me so I wrote my last
will on a bill of lading and a guard told Villa
I could write. He promoted me lieutenant colonel.

Siqueiros started laughing, picked up his chair
and sat back down.—*You were lucky.*
—*Always. So I was in on the taking of Zacatecas.*
It was a hairy business, I can tell you now,
Suarez laughed. *From Villa I learned not to be*
a mere thief but to aspire to be a gangster.
So things are not so black and white. But not to worry.
I won't abandon you. I'm like the air.
You'll have to take a breath . . . some time.

Siqueiros strode down the sidewalk
shaking his head back and forth, chuckling
at the thought of this merry pirate.
He passed a grocery. Boxes of chili, red, green,
yellow corn, hills of lemons, limes, the smell of them
wriggling up his nose. How to paint that?
How to paint being happy to be alive?

FRIDA'S GARDEN

She hobbled with Siqueiros
in her Tehuantepec princess dress
with embroidered Mayan glyphs,
her ivory-tipped cane clocking steps
on flagstone, shadows cast by her hips
like cam-wheels, over and down,
over and down, like her life.
An orange gash of evening ripped
slate-purple clouds. She asked him
how things were with his mural.

He told her he had the central image,
the minting press, the voodoo of money
that makes eyes bigger than stomachs,
that unbraids the tribal weave.
But what he badly needed was space,
time to let his soul sort the chaos.

Workmen ramped wheelbarrows
up planks to a small pyramid she was
having built in the garden corner
to coax the old gods out. Laborers
slapped mortar, tamped it with trowels,
measured with plumb-line and level.
He asked if Diego would party later.
—*Yes. There'll be plenty of tail for him to chase.*
He snatched up Frida's hand.
—*Join us in our march against Trotsky . . .*
Frida looked down at the flagstones.
—*I like that you paint metaphors. So do I.*
But I couldn't stab el Viejo in the back like that.
He wondered what she saw in Trotsky.

One workman turned to Frida.
She pressed a hundred pesos in his palm
then turned to David with a shrug.
—*His skin gives off a comforting Odessa light.*
The workmen disappeared through gates.

Siqueiros picked up a trowel, admiring its
taper, wielding it like a short sword.
—*Why would you give safe harbor to a traitor to*
                    everything you believe in?
Frida took the trowel from his hand.
—*It's my harbor. I'll give it to whomever I please.*

He picked up a brick, measuring its length
from his fingertips to the heel of his palm
as if to fling it through a bank window.
She took it from him, set it on the altar
to whatever made the sun rise.
—*How could you do it to poor Diego?* he asked.
Frida shoved him a hard one in the chest.
            —*Poor Diego?*

—*It's been a crazy day. Nightmares,*
then trouble with the law. The Colonel picked me up
to shake me down. I almost broke a bank window
got arrested, was bailed out in the third hour
by this gangster hotelier who wants me to paint his lobby . . .
Frida smirked.—*Try being married to a lovable disaster.*

Outside, on Londres Street, David jumped
back as military trucks carrying National Guardsmen
almost ran over him.
            —*Baby-faced killers,*
he muttered as he hurried off under the moon,
remembering Diego, Frida, like a ceramic Tree of Life
with fruit in saints' and angels' forms, and, wrapped
around the trunk,
            the serpent of wanting different things.

MAY DAY

Constitution Plaza

A fifty-foot flag pole with huge silk
Mexican flag rippled in breezes, hundreds
massed for the manifestation, mariachis
in *charro* costumes played bright spring morning.
David, Angelica, Adrianna, and Luis among
throngs eager as track stars for the gun to sound.
Contreras, all smiles.—*What a crowd! What a day!*
Will we make the headlines? he asked Angelica.

When she shrugged, he turned to David:
We want you, our famous painter, to lead the march.
—*Oh, so now he's your 'famous painter.'* Angelica scolded.
—*He's not such a bargain, your 'famous painter.'*
You know we had to kick your wild man out of the party.
—*You kicked me out the door,* Siqueiros snapped,
        but I climbed back in the window.

Contreras blew his whistle, marshals formed the crowd,
flags, pennants, banners hoisted aloft.
        MEXICO, SI! TROTSKY, NO!
Angelica handed Adrianna to David, stepped out,
shot a flash as the march took its first step.
advancing along government buildings,
turning toward cathedral gates.

Military trucks roared up to block the plaza.
National Guardsmen jumped down, formed phalanxes,
        their rifles fitted with obsidian blades.
They were wearing gas masks like in his painting,
so many, they surrounded the marchers, moved in,
stamping boots, firing shots overhead. Angels
fell from the sky, hit pavement without a thud,
their trumpets and halos dented.

The crowd broke ranks.
Groups sprinted from street to street, each exit
blocked by trucks, the crowd herded down side alleys
into soldiers' nets, hustled into police vans.
Contreras shouted to a soldier.—*How can you
do this, Carlos? It's me, uncle Ramon!*
Rifle-butted, Contreras went down, face bloody.

More shots fired, screams. Red banners fell fluttering.
—*The Colonel warned me,* Siqueiros whispered to Angelica.
—*What?* she asked as he grabbed her hand,
picked up Adrianna, raced into the cathedral.
Under its vast nave Mass was being sung.
He saw a red Satan hovering above the faithful,
black claws clutching Romanesque arches.

The priest turned to face the people
intoning *"orate frates,"* startled to see refugees
charging down center aisle pursued by tear gas outside.
A shaft of color shone through stained windows,
clouds of incense shrouded a life-sized Jesus
pointing to his heart which hovered somehow
in the air an inch from his robe the same as
the still-beating sacrifice of an Aztec.
—*Do you seek sanctuary?* the priest asked.
—*Only passage,* Siqueiros answered.
Angelica crossed herself:—*We may be communists
but we're Mexican communists and we believe in God.*

The priest unlocked the rail.
They ran up steps, around the altar,
past the carved stone gods that had survived
four hundred years by the grace of whatever
spirits guard them, made their way
through sacristy, doorway, sunlight, street,
hailed a taxi, sped off
          just as the jaws were closing.

CATHEDRAL

Night

Pockets of darkness in side chapels,
quiet as intervals between drips hitting
cisterns. *Plop!* Echoes of a match struck
to light candles, where Siqueiros saw Satan
sleeping upside-down, a giant bat with
Mayan stars painted on his wings
and heaven counting on Venus clocks.
The confessional booth's oak door creaked
on hinges sticky as ancient sins. He knelt
from habit. The screen slid with a slick hiss
oiled by two billion tears of contrition.
—*Perfect place to meet, mais no?*
Here in the birthing house of death's author?
David said nothing.
You saw the real face of your government,
the foreigner's beard behind the President's hand?
He heard the invisible voice, a claw scratch
telling him to gather a team, to attack Trotsky's house,
to make it seem an operation led by Almazán,
to burn Trotsky's book about Stalin, but not kill him.
 —*We have other plans for that*, the voice said.
        Go then, and sin no more.
—*Don't blaspheme,* David whispered, *it's bad luck.*
A folded map slipped beneath the confessional door.
When he stepped out of the booth
there was no one, not even a footfall's echo.
nothing but the vast interior space.

ZONA ROSA

Off the nightclub beat
a rooster scratched a mound of dead grass
in a dark warren of alleyways.
Fire escapes dripped with recent showers.
Who knew what scum lay in shadows
waiting to jump him for his cash?
The guns were easy. The ammunition
and the clips in the right caliber would be hard.
He breathed deeply as he mounted
the wooden and uncertain stairs
the same way he painted, by muscling his way,
each step a token of the stroke by stroke
impulse to *do something,* even if it's wrong.
that pushed him on.
        On the seventh floor was
the red light the Chinaman said would signal him.
He climbed past back-porch baby carriages,
trash barrels, bicycles,
        looked down into the blackness.
Vertigo twinged behind his knees.
He told himself it was not that he wanted to jump,
but that he needed the edge to find
what was truly his to give.
He heard a cry—long, piercing, final.

What if something had happened to Angelica?
He knocked on the door. It creaked ajar.
A cloud of red neon light leaked into the room
onto a man with a Pacific blue sapphire
filling one empty eye socket.
The door clicked shut behind him.
The silence floated in its inert menace.
He sensed he was not alone with the Chinaman.
He stood still, his body clenched as a gun muzzle's
frosted zero burned the back of his neck.

The Chinaman's one eye read his guest's face.
—*You're a cold fish,* he chuckled.
There were six machine-pistol clips on the table
boxed in cardboard for a concealed carry.
I have made these myself, came the voice, *with a few extra grains . . .*
    you have the money?
Siqueiros set a roll of bills on the table.
The Chinaman picked it up, felt its heft.
My assistant will show you the way out.
Turning toward the door with the box, Siqueiros said,
—*I wish he could.*

FAREWELL TO SAN ANGEL

The guitarist sounded like a combo
the way he strummed and struck staccato
with his thumb on his rosewood sound-box.
A crowd of friends jammed into Diego's parlor.
Siqueiros felt the urge to dance, to give
Tina Modoti a twirl. He sat there instead
with Diego sipping tequila and watching Frida
amazingly spin as if without shattered pelvis,
her fingertips brushing Tina's nipples.
He could have sat there forever beside Diego,
a figure in a Pompei fresco
holding a symposium on sexual fire
never mentioning the insistent Sr. Suarez y Suarez
nor how he thought Diego better suited
to decorating a hotel lobby with perhaps
three girls in pastel one-piece bathing suits
lounging on a deck overlooking Acapulco,
an ad really, prompting impromptu flights.
He remained silent. Who knew what
Diego would do if he took insult in the debate
over the decorative and the illustrative?
Perhaps he would produce a hip cannon
which he would fire into the ceiling,
an exclamation point causing plaster to
rain on the dancers, causing the dancers to
flee screaming into the night, ending the party.
Siqueiros had no wish for the party to end.
Tina challenged him to a drinking duel.
He took two deep swallows, but there was
the mission to think of. He had to stay sober.
He took one last long look at the dancers,
then walked out onto the balcony alone.
In the distance he saw Trotsky's house
going to sleep one light at a time.

The darkness held the question: not "if,"
but "how" his life would change. There's
always a carcass for the vulture, he thought.

COYOACÁN

From a second-story Victrola
flamenco music cascaded onto Vienna Street.
Segovia's nimble fingers trickled down like rain off tiles.
Balcony lights bubbled onto jacaranda walls.

Siqueiros plucked a rose from a trellis,
skipped up the rain-slicked staircase, slipped
his arm around Julia Serrano's waist,
she who'd been tempting Trotsky's guards
for a week now, promising her charms.

Luis and a half-dozen men clapped
to the beat, passing a goatskin of wine
as David spun her into a dance step,
rose in teeth, stamping boots into hardwood,
two fingers to his forehead like horns,
making a pass in his grandfather's arena.

She, now the matador, swirling skirts for cape,
miming a torero spinning in a Veronica.
wanted to be in on the kill as the music climaxed.

Julia ran to the kitchen and returned
with opened boxes of army and police uniforms.
Luis and the other men dove in like kids at a costume party.
She left and returned, this time with machine pistols in her arms.
He asked them to stand with him once more.
With artillery fire still in their heads,
with letters from family still bleeding news of friends
shot by Franco's army, they listened.
—*You're here for an affair of exceptional importance,*
        an attack on Trotsky's house.
—*About time!* David's soldiers shouted.

KILLING TIME

3 AM, May 24, 1940, Coyoacán, Mexico

Siqueiros rode shotgun in Luis' sedan
as raindrops fell like olives from ripened orchards.
      Oscillating wipers divided time
into blurred streetlight diamonds and static
on the yellow radio face,
              four hundred years
from the murals he was born to paint that
would strip the flags of revolutionary glory
      and un-conceal the death march.

He held his sketch of Trotsky's compound
to the weak light of the radio, checking again
its guardhouse, machine-gun nest.
A nut tough to crack.

To thunder's sonata in blackness
the car's high beams froze an armadillo,
its eyes sulfur reflectors as it crossed a street
strewn with palm branches. Luis
swerved to avoid it.
         The car fishtailed
triggering a clench in David's gut.
The clock said 3:51 AM.

A canvas-covered truck splashed past their car.
Siqueiros turned to Luis, pointed his chin
at two rows of National Guardsmen inside.
A campesino with the look of every local Jesus
      pulled his burro through a gutter wave.
Siqueiros could see in the old man's eyes
curtains on a windowless wall. He guessed that
for him it was rain and it came from God.

Bumping over potholes the car felt back-heavy
        as if there were a corpse in the trunk.
He gestured for Luis to stop, ran across
sidewalks to cover the old man with a trench coat
he'd worn since Barcelona, that lake of blood.

Back in the car he saw the old man
cover his animal with the coat.
A chill shivered in him. He could give his gift,
but he couldn't know how it would be used.
What if the people he painted for
never saw the world he created?
In an alley a coyote, all hackled angles,
        shook a shower from its fur.

He drove by Frida's indigo walls,
flipped his cigarette out the window,
followed its arc until it sizzled in the black
puddle of his mother's lungs after her last breath.
What darkness had she vanished into taking with her
the song about selling shoes to angels?
What if he could turn it back to before?

He had once believed he had come
into the world to hunt her after-traces,
to establish the reign of angels.
He tried for years to ease the miners' pain
for the crime of not dying enough
to make up for all the blisters and hunger,
raising his voice against a sky with no dawn
after two wrecked loves
        he felt he'd never survive,
and in the muffler music rumbling down
Coyoacán's arteries he heard himself wonder
what am I doing here . . .
        as he turned onto Vienna Street
what came to him was the music of bed creak,

love moan, bird cry, war dance, seed time,
struggle-in-the-street song, his hands
beautiful as lilacs over stretch-marked canvas
through places and times that drove through him,
that drove him through, that swirled him
back to where this night all started,

and in the muffler music rumbling down
Coyoacán's arteries he heard himself wonder
what am I doing here . . .

TROTSKY COMPOUND

24 May 1940

Siqueiros drove through a pre-dawn rain
        that purified Vienna Street
remembering his mother's death, a young man
under a foreman's whip, a lake of blood
on a plaza in Barcelona,
        and whose side he was on.
He heard Suarez y Suarez say
an artist shouldn't be on anybody's side.
—*What bullshit,* he muttered to himself.
—*What?* Luis asked, glancing.

The rain shut off, the tires went on
hissing as they coasted, lights off,
the last fifty feet toward Trotsky's castle
with its turrets, machine-gun nest,
flood-lights pooling beyond the stucco wall
on the center courtyard.
—*Look at how the man is barricaded.*
He's so rich from selling his soul to the North Americans
        even the Devil calls him collect.

Everyone piled out of the car.
Siqueiros knocked on the guardhouse door.
—*Snap inspection!* Two policemen stepped outside
buttoning tunics, rubbing little-boy eyes.
Luis and Nestor pistol-whipped them back to sleep.
Julia jingled the gate bell.
        Evaporating rain
steamed from each angle of the fortress.
Stillness curled a claw about the sleeping castle.
She sang through a crack in the double doors:
—*It's me, Roberto. I need your love tonight.*
Roberto unlocked the gate.

Luis put a pistol to the kid's head,
hustled him into the trunk, locked it.

The team fanned out into the garden.
Siqueiros gave the nod and the staccato of
spraying bullets punctured the silence.
Strings of holes pocked stucco walls like notes of music.
Above, in the pill-box, machine guns opened fire,
tracers ricocheted off fountain and flagstone
         walkways, cutting flowers in half.

A shrill shriek inside the house.
A man's silhouette in a bedroom.
—*The son of a bitch wants to die,* Luis shouted.
He raised his weapon. David pulled it down.
—*I had him in my sights,* Luis whined.
—*We're soldiers, not murderers.*

Thermos bombs clanged on stucco,
their fuses spit sparks, spurts of flame.
Luis took one in the leg, went down on a knee.
—*Viva Almazán!* he shouted as David
hoisted him up and hopped him into the car,
blowing his whistle for the rest to pile in
and roar off. Gone in an eye-blink.

CAMPOS ELISEOS

Luis drove off through the fog,
his engine whirring up through its gears,
tearing the dawn stillness like dry parchment.
Machine-gun fire still rang in Siqueiros' ears.
His focus had broken him into two drunks
on the sidewalk sleeping as if dead, without flies.
A millennial breath sighed through daybreak.
Brakes screeched; a dog yipped. When he blinked
his eyes felt like there were fish hooks in his lids.
Through the bruised crack of the east
the sun was the stump of a three-legged mutt
carrying news that Trotsky wasn't his only
or even his main enemy but Mexico's histories
and that the logical end of his rebellion
left him with nothing
but the broken mouth of the cynically insane.
It was more than he could paint.

Angelica came out of the house in a bathrobe
with a pair of clippers and a flower vase.
He took his military tunic off and tossed it in the trash.
—*Destroying the evidence?* she asked.
—*The bombs didn't explode.*
And now there are too many tongues to wag.
—*Anyone hurt?*
—*Luis took one in the leg.*
—*Ai!* Angelica's vase cracked on the slate walkway.
Four plainclothesmen drove up in a black Buick,
stopped, ran out of the car with guns pulled.
—*Who are they?*
—*Cardenas' men come to make me pay for crossing him.*
—*Wherever you're going, I'm going . . . to look out for you.*
He hugged her quick, then frowned.
—*Killing a woman is nothing to these bastards.*
Angelica pulled him into their car parked behind the house.

She jammed it in reverse and gunned it north
weaving through trees, then headed
for the rotary at Elysian Fields.
The .45 was still there in the glove compartment.
Gunshots smashed the rear window.
Cold air bit their hands.
—*What about Adrianna?* he yelled.
—*My family* . . . Angelica pulled another right
onto Hegel then hit the gas toward Ruben Darío.
A bullet broke the rear mirror inside the car.
Falling glass cut her driving hand.
When she licked the blood she lost control
and crashed into an iron gate. She stumbled up
the stairs into an apartment building.
He gestured to say he would call, then ran
in his suspenders across the street named for the poet
who sang of Nicaragua's magical nights,
then through the Bosque to a bus at his Paseo stop.
He got on, scrunched down and got away unseen.
When he got to his friend's house he saw
a pigeon take flight from a copper-green rooftop.
He would have liked that very much, to launch
into a source of joy and disappear.

FLIGHT

To make good their escape he shed
his jeans and turtleneck for peasant's clothes,
she changed into a cotton blouse and skirt.
His straw sombrero haloed him as he hacked
through mesquite bramble with machete
scrambling up and down Sisyphean hills
remembering the magazine he, Diego, and Orozco
used to publish as he sang, one slash per accent:
> *The machete serves to cut the cane*
> *to open paths in forests*
> *to cut the heads off rattlesnakes*
> *and slash the heartless rich . . .*
one stroke every day for four hundred years.
Angelica's skirt, cactus thorn shreds now,
noon clouds coming from Colima's volcanic plume.

The baying came closer.
Years since he roved Jalisco's mountains
organizing a union for miners, hiding in root cellars
as police dogs sniffed and women stood silently
fuming at the insult from strangers
tearing their kitchens apart,
the hounds of Tlaloc or Jehovah come to collect
the tithe that's paid in blood labor
to make the sun rise, brewing the next spell of hunger,
the next house lost. the next child, the last ounce,
until all that's left is defiance and chipped flint.

He took Angelica's hand,
scrambled past saguaros flowered red
that stood like ancient wall paintings of Aztec teachers
from whose mouths flowed the sacred words
that showed the difference between the true artist
and the carrion artist, who cheats the people with lies.

They climbed to a cave opening,
Inside, a pool they fell into, splashing faces,
taking long drinks, rolling onto their backs, reading
names scrawled on cave walls until his eyes closed . . .

he was walking down a dry wash
under an autumn sun with Don Antonio and Eusebia.
They climbed a barranca studded with agave,
cactus, cholla, mesquite brush,
where orange butterflies sipped nectar from *ocotillos*.
Don Antonio winked at David.
—*They come from el Norte like tourists to mate.*
See how they dance like ballerinas?
On their wings is painted the faces of their souls,
every sunset of their brief lives, every generation
            back to the first butterflies.
The ancient ones saw them as angels of nature,
carrying off souls of the dying. In their picture writing
the teacher's lesson is carnations blooming from his mouth.
Colossal sorcerers fell during the Conquest.
They were Titans. We are ants in comparison.
Are you ready to take the power to destroy and create?

David wants the most perfect one,
to gild it, mount it on a pin, give it to Eusebia.
His grandfather tells him to circle up
and flush them down so she can make the capture.
It's a good plan, and the boy tells him so.
What's an old man for, Don Antonio says,
if not to teach his grandson the tricks men have known
            since the earth was still wet?

David scrambles up, gets behind the butterflies:
Ai! Ai! he shouts. And as they flutter
down the dusty draw Eusebia cries: *Oh, my God!*
He runs back down. Don Antonio lies, clutching his chest,
face purple.

Eusebia kneels beside him,
smiling down into his face. Already beyond help,
Don Antonio begs David with his last breath:
Bring back the Titans, David, bring back the age of giants.
A hundred butterflies cluster around his face.

Siqueiros woke with a sharp pain in his ribs.
—*Hands up, you son of a bitch!*
The other policeman wrangled a brace of berserk dogs.
The first threw him face-down on rocks,
pulled his hands back, cuffing him.
Blood from his split eyebrow dripped into the pool,
raying out like sprays of pink pyroxylin.
—*Is this what they pay you for?*
—*Shut up!*
—*Or what?* Angelica shouted,
picking up the machete, smacking him
with the flat side across the back.
He fired his pistol at her feet near David's head,
        the powder flash searing his eyes.
The other cop let out enough leash
to set the dogs on her, their teeth tearing her ankles.
She cried out, as David rolled in the pool,
his hands covering his eyes.
—*For God's sake, he's a painter!*

BY OTHER MEANS

1

His neck rope-burned raw
from policemen yanking him to jail.
He heard townspeople flinging doors open
milling on the plaza. A women's voice shouted.
—*It's the union man!*
Siqueiros guessed it must be Hostotipaquillo.
He smelled an orange torn apart, sweet acid on parched lips.
He heard Angelica licking juice.
The mob laid hands on him, lifted him
off the pavement, whether to free him or rip him apart
he could not tell. A squad car siren screamed.
He heard the bustling crowd back off.
—*I'll take them from here.*
—*You'll have to sign.* Flash-bulbs popped!
He could see that much. It was a good omen.

On the flight from Guadalajara
he lost track of where he was. Pushed,
shoved up flights of stairs, footsteps crunched
on pea-stone, sun on his face. Hands and arms
turned him upside-down, hung him by his legs.
A drop of blood dripped off his nose.
He heard it splat seconds later on the sidewalk.
Who ordered you to attack Trotsky's house?
—*No one. I've wanted him out of Mexico a long time.*
You want me to believe the attack was your idea?
          You think I'm a fool?
—*Well, then, don't ask stupid questions.*
—*Why don't you just paint your damn pictures*
          and mind your own business?

The policemen let him slip from calves to ankles.
They hugged his feet closer to their chests,
their badges scraping his skin.

Then a voice he recognized.
—*Pull that man up!*
He felt himself hauled like a net full of crabs.
Do you know who he is? the Colonel asked the sergeant.
—*A subversive. A threat to Mexico.*
—*A world-famous artist. The President-elect's friend.*
The Colonel draped his tunic over David's shoulders.

2

Shadows with teeth,
gray clouds that might be people moving
in what he was told was the Hall of Justice.
Nervous coughing, scuffling feet, traffic noise outside.
—*Remember the old saying,* the Judge advised,
          if you represent yourself, you'll have a fool for a lawyer.

Siqueiros faced the voice, felt his breath in long
crimson scrolls accuse Trotsky of subverting Mexico.
—*But as the government would not act,*
he said, trying to fill his voice with probity
a citizen's arrest was in order.
His hired thugs resisted, gun-fire ensued and
except for a couple of flesh wounds no harm was done.
He heard the Judge chuckle, then a gavel bang.
—*There is of course the kidnapping and murder of*
the north American, Robert Sheldon Harte, to account for.
Defendant is remanded without bail as a flight risk.
—*What!* Siqueiros cried.
A hand grabbed his elbow.
He bumped into furniture, turned his head
toward Adrianna's voice. All he could see was
something like waves, all he could hear was a rustling
in the crowd of reporters rushing to telephones.
He smelled the Colonel's cigarette
as he was taken from the bailiff's hands,
heard the click of door latches as he was led.

A blur behind a desk spoke.

—*Remember a rainy night during the last days of the revolution?*

A young lieutenant the other officers refused a place to sleep?

He remembered a tent filled with snoring.

He was dreaming of riding through Oaxaca,

of temples with bright yellow parrots, purple jaguars.

—*Avila Camacho?*

—*President-Elect.*

—*Should I offer congratulations or condolences?*

—*I don't want you in prison on my watch.*

I've made some back channel arrangements for you . . .

—*And my family?*

—*. . . can live with you in Chile until this noise dies down.*

He felt a piece of paper stuffed in his hand.

Go to this address. The Colonel dressed him

in what could only be a priest's cassock and papal hat.

—*And I will forego my day in court because?*

—*Because despite appearance to the contrary you are a patriot.*

CHILEAN CONSULATE

Siqueiros' eyes made out an old servant
in white jacket leading him, Angelica and Adrianna
into a room lit by a green-shaded lamp.
A recording softly played violins and accordion
squeezing out the slow pulse of a tango.
A figure rose to its full height, a bear standing.
—*Is that David Siqueiros beneath a papal hat?*
A paw extended across the circle of light.
My name is Pablo Neruda.
I wish we could have met under better circumstances.
But we're rebels, he chuckled, *and what can we expect?*
I've learned to travel light, a pen, a notebook,
some clean underwear and my beat-up integrity.
Siqueiros heard the smack of a kiss on Angelica's hand,
then he felt the weight of a warm paw on his shoulder
—*The Judas Trotsky is less injured than you, my friend.*
—*All I need is a wall to paint,* he said to the shape.
He tried to explain why he couldn't kill Trotsky,
              but his voice died on the carpet.
He heard Pablo shuffle stacks of paper,
felt papers slipped into his hands.
—*These will get you to Chile where there's a commission.*
He could think of no way to thank Pablo but hugging.
—*Ugh,* Pablo said, *I never thought I'd hug a priest.*
Pablo held Siqueiros at arm's length.
What you hoped would happen to Trotsky will now happen to you,
he supposed. *Here, a toy for you,* he chirped to Adrianna.
David heard the clack of ball on a string into cup.

NOON AT THE EQUATOR

1

Strapped into seats, tight buckles
their ears drilled by the DC-3's roar,
their blood and cell fibers oxygen-starved,
Siqueiros' eyesight restored enough to guess
the distance narrowing between aluminum wings
and granite peaks like snowy teeth
reaching to rip the plane's fuselage as it
sputtered over ice fields inches from crash,

Adrianna buried her face in her father's chest.
He smoothed her hair, hummed a tuneless tune.
The co-pilot lurched back. smiled,
pointing to a stack of boxes
opened the cargo door   air whooshed out!
Adrianna's, Angelica's hair flew.
The co-pilot motioned Siqueiros to help him
        toss boxes out

each carton dropped was an inch gained
then, just past the stone daggers slicing the sky
        green valleys,
irrigation ditches, Bolivia.   crops
and in a minute checking through Customs
        the uniformed Security Officer
            —*Papers, please.*
—*Is there a problem?* Siqueiros asked.
             —*These aren't valid.*
—*But they were authorized by a consular official.*
—*Yes, but the Ambassador himself has rescinded them,*
        as you are in unlawful flight.

Angelica raised her voice.—*I have a child to care for!*
—*You're not under arrest. Only protective custody.*
Many Trotskyites live here. They want to get their hands on you.

As such you are a threat to public order.
We've arranged a hotel room as you make plans to leave.

2 HOTEL LA PAZ

Beyond the balcony, the Andes.
Adrianna sat on the floor
playing with her cup-string-and-ball toy.
Siqueiros matched the snowy mountains to Angelica's
lithe topography stretched out on the bed
in her white dress, shoes and stockings.
He paced between the balcony and the regency dresser
distracted by the crowd at the pool chanting
　　　　"Assassin! Assassin!"

The man at the door in a seersucker suit
handed "Senora" a card with a bow:
　　　　HECTOR MARTINEZ
　　　　MEXICAN CONSUL
—I have good news, sort of?
President Camacho has explained to President Cerda
that you are commissioned to paint a mural as a goodwill gift
　　　　between the Mexican and Chilean peoples.
—The catch?
—No such agreement exists between Mexico and Bolivia.
　　　　—"Assassin! Assassin!"
—Trotsky's been murdered. A grisly affair, he shuddered,
struck in the head with a mountaineer's ice-axe . . .
They think you did it.
Siqueiros glanced at Angelica.
So that was the "other plan" his contact
hinted at when he whispered his instructions for the raid.
He gazed out the balcony window.
—"Assassin! Assassin!" the crowd below chanted.
He had to get his family away from here to safety.
—How far is Chile? he asked Hector Martinez,
who raised his arm and pointed to the south.
He gazed at the mountains.
The Andes were so close.

72

MOUNTAIN ROAD AT SNOWLINE

Hector Martinez jammed his car
in reverse, his tires inscribed an arc in the road's
gravel. and he raced back to the city below,
leaving Siqueiros, Angelica and Adrianna,
trudging calf-deep in snow toward a jagged pass
with raincoats, blankets, surgical masks
one foot in front of the other as the wind
whipped snow into white-outs, no shadows,
a white disc above fists of sleet pounding them
every step until they stumbled into a cave mouth
and a supper of frozen chocolate bars.

The squall screwed itself into the ice,
the setting sun threw down long red rays,
a dance of fiery veils arcing toward night,
a sea of radium lava in the blood
casting vague shapes on cave walls
condensed to stars in the bowl of night.
—*This is what I've always wanted.* Siqueiros said.
—*To live in a cave?* Angelica asked with a frosted grin.
He picked Adrianna up in his arms.
—*The first paintings are found in caves.*
He settled her on the cave floor, piling clothes
blankets into a bed for her, then leaned on the wall
to watch the snow-swirl churn to sculpted dunes.
He saw himself there, a single flake blown
among billions into the impasse of mountain spires.
He knelt at the cave mouth, exhausted,
as the last flare burst upon the peaks.
He raised his head and arms.

All his life he had dreamed of the people free.
He knew now it wouldn't happen in his lifetime.

—I see it now, the shrine I always wanted,
the monument to those in the future who will finally enjoy,
not just the fruits of their labor, but the liberty to create . . .
He stood and with the light still left
began moving his arm, sketching shapes
inscribing on the cave like the interior of a skull,
of a brain, fixing in his muscles the steady
curving fluid line of forms, women pruning
the tree of life, men carrying babies, their bodies
at peace in the eternal motion of harvest.

SCHOOL HOUSE IN CHILLAN, CHILE

On a scaffold Siqueiros drew down
three black streaks on Cuahtémoc's left cheek,
final strokes on his masque of sacrifice
in the shock of combat as if the hash of mangled
body parts, shattered spears, and bloody flag
in the hands of Bernardo O'Higgins were magma
forcing up through the fissures of battle into
the next great volcano.
                              The last Aztec king's
severed hands were proof that his warning to
Cuernavaca's people was true. Like Mexico Chile
ripped itself from Spain's arms yet still staggered,
trailing its afterbirth, wounded, two races,
blond-haired, black-haired, turning the din of war
to starlight shining behind Siqueiros' eyes.

Angelica asked him to turn to the camera.
She saw his face was streaked like Cuahtémoc's.

As the children clustered in the corner, their heads
tilted to see the painting, mouths gaped open.
Angelica took their picture. Her camera
panned toward the conic form on the ceiling
that made the painting seem fourteen feet high.

The school principal handed Siqueiros a telegram.
He ripped it open, read. Turned to Angelica.
—*We can go home now.*
—*To face prosecution, prison?* she asked.
He stepped into the doorway, imagining
waves on beaches outside Conceptión, white
mists combed back by sea breezes
and the first step onto a ship docked atTalcuhuano
to sail them back to Coyoacán where he would
visit the grave of Diego's friend, Trotsky.

He dared not hope to be acquitted,
though he had no hand in Sheldon Harte's death.
Caged how long this time?
Perhaps they would let him paint.
Even Hell can be livable, as long as it's home.

SPIRAL SHELLS IN THE BLACK PALACE

Lecumberri Prison, 24 November 1963

A guard's iambic footsteps woke him.
Siqueiros swung his legs over the side of the bunk,
scratched his ribs. smoothed his feathery hair.

The guard asked if he'd heard the young
north American President's head was blown
apart. He added his surprise
    that it hadn't happened
sooner to the rich man's son who thought he
could change the world as he reached through
the cell bars to light
   the prisoner's cigarette stub.

The match flash illuminated a lined face,
a father's silver cross glinted on his denim shirt.
Moonlight through his barred window
threw a shadow on two paintings on the wall.
One, his portrait of Angelica, her skin, white
Castilian rose, arms like Athena's, solacing breasts,
green eyes that held nothing back,
her red lips just about to whisper, *I remember*
a fiesta in white, green, red strips of crepe
strung on brick walls of a Los Angeles restaurant,
Christmas lights hanging from street lamps,
young families dancing.
    He drew a line of
fresh white acrylic onto a palette as cigarette
smoke stung his eyes, made him squint as ashes fell.

He smiled them in with a tooth brush palette knife
coughed, applied another stroke to a self portrait
his hand nail-scratched
the fourth wall

between him and whoever, whatever dared
to look between himself
        and himself just beyond,
ripping through whatever kept him
begging the question of inside or outside,
that kept him revising Angelica's impossible

beauty elusive as freedom behind bars,
secret as dreams that tell him
prison is not about space.

He would have liked to calm his heart,
whose jaw is a wire bird-cage crying envy
against the zero of gravestones.
He knew the freedom he sought would not
occur in his lifetime.
        Again, he reached into his magician's
hat for the sketch-pad and charcoal to limn out
that Judas kiss in the heart of everyone,

the fantastic jaguar painting that devours
its painter, a man with a phantom twin
blooming from his sternum.
He stopped measuring the dimensions of his cell.
He began sketching spirits, ghosts, prophecies.
Stars hung like hummingbirds above trumpet vines.
The blossom arrived. History was assassinated.
Lightning revealed the musculature of clouds
and he remembered that barkeep in Barcelona
and imagined him walking home through scattered
gunfire as he entered his kitchen, pulled the light cord,
saw a cricket under his table.

POLYFORUM

Sunday afternoon, 1975

Fathers in white shirts and striped ties,
mothers in Sunday dresses gone to Mass
and this afternoon, admission free.

They have entered the immense cave
to be swallowed by images flickering on its walls,
bending back to see the ceiling's apex

with astronaut and cosmonaut
suspended in orbit, opening the future,
the children asking questions, parents

pointing to details, a golden gyre
spinning destiny from dynamos Siqueiros
imagined years before in Central Park

throbbing *woom, woom, woom*
its spires and spindles source and center of
celestial hummingbirds . . . and at eye-level

those who hasten to join the storm
where some spirit, ready to attack as they sleep
beneath the poisoned tree . . . the people

surrounded by its walls, a mother as she looks up
whispering,—*Él debe haber tenido
una mente brillante y un espíritu de paz.*

Through every barrier humanity marches
across an earth spinning into the dark rift
where the galaxy opens its center

to sun and earth spinning in its light,
a human whose chrysalis body releases its future
that once was bound in service to a machine,

restless as electricity forking to ground,
though its eyes look outward to families,
their voices raised against what tightens

around them even as they choose to spend
a Sunday afternoon, and
                        among the ghostly
gods in their heights to kiss the skull of un-

answering skies, wriggling from their silk
husks with black fires inside them,
                        an old
peasant leads a burro through street-lit rain.

BILL TREMBLAY is author of seven collections of poems, including *Crying in the Cheap Seats* (University of Massachusetts Press), *Duhamel* (BOA Editions), and *Shooting Script: Door of Fire* (Eastern Washington University Press). His novel, *The June Rise,* was published by Utah State University Press. He was one of the founders of the MFA program at Colorado State University where he was also, for many years, editor of the *Colorado Review,* and where he was recipient of the John F. Stern Distinguished Professor Award. He has also been awarded fellowships from the National Endowment for the Arts, the National Endowment for the Humanities, Yaddo, and the Fulbright Foundation. His poems have appeared in the Pushcart Prize anthology and in *Best American Poetry, 2003,* as well as in dozens of literary journals, including *Massachusetts Review, Manoa, Indiana Review, Ohio Review, Willow Springs, Michigan Quarterly Review, The Midwest Quarterly,* and many others. He lives with his wife, Cynthia, in Fort Collins, Colorado.